ŽIE

Ziefert, Harriet.

A polar bear can
swim.

$13.89   Preschool   10/26/1998

DATE			

A Polar Bear Can Swim

What Animals Can and Cannot Do

A Viking Science Easy-to-Read

by Harriet Ziefert
illustrated by Emily Bolam

VIKING

VIKING
Published by the Penguin Group
Penguin Putnam Inc., 375 Hudson Street, New York, New York 10014, U.S.A.
Penguin Books Ltd, 27 Wrights Lane, London W8 5TZ, England
Penguin Books Australia Ltd, Ringwood, Victoria, Australia
Penguin Books Canada Ltd, 10 Alcorn Avenue, Toronto, Ontario, Canada M4V 3B2
Penguin Books (N.Z.) Ltd, 182-190 Wairau Road, Auckland 10, New Zealand

Penguin Books Ltd, Registered Offices: Harmondsworth, Middlesex, England

First published in 1998 by Viking, a member of Penguin Putnam Books for Young Readers
Published simultaneously in Puffin Books

1 3 5 7 9 10 8 6 4 2

LIBRARY OF CONGRESS CATALOGING-IN-PUBLICATION DATA
Ziefert, Harriet.
A polar bear can swim : what animals can and cannot do / by Harriet Ziefert ;
illustrated by Emily Bolam.
p. cm. — (A Viking science easy-to-read)
Summary: Discusses the abilities and habits of a variety of
animals, including the polar bear, bat, and honeybee.
ISBN 0-670-88056-6
1. Animals—Miscellanea—Juvenile literature. [1. Animals—
Miscellanea.] I. Bolam, Emily, ill. II. Title. III. Series.
QL49.Z486 1998 590—DC21 97-27542 CIP AC

Printed in Hong Kong
Set in Bookman

Reading level 2.3

A Polar Bear Can Swim

A polar bear can swim.

A polar bear can dive under the ice.

A polar bear can sleep curled up.

But a polar bear can't sleep
upside down.

A bat can sleep upside down.

A bat can catch 600 insects
in an hour.

A bat can fly in the dark
without bumping into things.

But a bat can't fly backward.
A hummingbird can fly backward.

A hummingbird can beat its wings
faster than any other bird.

A hummingbird
can reach deep into
a flower with its long beak.

But a hummingbird can't sting.
A honeybee can sting.

A honeybee can buzz.

A honeybee can make honey.

But a honeybee can't make milk.
A cow can make milk.

A cow can drink 75 gallons
of water in a day.

A cow can eat 100 pounds of grass

and poop 15 times in one day.

But a cow can't spout.
A whale can spout.

A whale can sing.
A whale can use its tail to jump.

But a whale can't hop.
A kangaroo can hop.

A kangaroo can carry her
baby, or joey, in a pouch.

A kangaroo can box.

But a kangaroo can't fly.
A toucan can fly.

A toucan can make loud noises.

A toucan can hide in the jungle.

But a toucan can't swim.

A polar bear can swim!

Science Fun

1. Choose one of the animals in the book and learn about some other things it can do. Make a list. For example:

> *A bear can climb.*
> *A bear can fish.*
> *A bear can find honey.*

2. Be a copycat. Make your own book, just like this one. Here are some animals to choose from: cheetah, sloth, penguin, giant tortoise, crocodile, python, camel. Draw a picture and write a sentence about each. For example:

> *An ostrich can't fly.*
> *But a bluebird can fly.*

Since this is a big project, you may want to do this with a friend.